Mrs. Allen
5th Grade

TARNISHED LEGACY
The Story of the Comstock Lode

by Ellen Hopkins

Perfection Learning®

Dedication

To those working to make our world a better place.

About the Author

Ellen Hopkins lives with her family, four dogs, two cats, and three tanks of fish near Carson City, Nevada. A California native, Ellen moved to the Sierra Nevada to ski. While writing for a Lake Tahoe newspaper, she discovered many exciting things and fascinating people.

Acknowledgements

Mae Gustin, John Warwick, Paul Lechler, Mark Warren

Image Credits: Bettmann/Corbis p. 5; Dave G. Houser/Corbis p. 47; Michael T. Sedam/Corbis pp. 57, 58; Phil Schermeister/Corbis p. 32; Corbis pp. 12, 26, 38, 39, 41; Bancroft Library, University of California, Berkeley pp. 25, 42, 45, 59; Denver Public Library pp. 49, 55

Library of Congress pp. 2, 3, 11, 14, 18, 20, 21, 24, 29, 35, 40, 52, 53; Corel p. 16; IMSI MasterPhotos p. 10; some images copyright www.arttoday.com

Cover and Book Design: Alan D. Stanley
Illustration: Alan D. Stanley pp. 13, 36

Table of Contents

Introduction

The Richest Little City in the West

Nevada. What does this word make you think of? Las Vegas. Bright lights. Casinos. Golf courses. Swimming pools. All swallowed up by hot desert sand.

Today, Las Vegas is a happening place. But 150 years ago, it was just an outpost called The Springs. The "action" was farther north, in a town called Virginia City.

You thought Virginia City was a ghost town? Not exactly. She does have her ghosts. At least if you listen to people who live there. They say you can hear spurs *chink* against the empty boardwalk. You can see will-o'-the-wisps behind unlit windows. You can smell cigar smoke in unoccupied rooms.

Is Virginia City haunted? Maybe. If so, her spirits belong to the miners, soldiers, outlaws, and silver barons who lived and died in the richest little city in the West.

This is their story.

Chapter 1

The Rush to Gold

The California Gold Rush

January 1848. James Marshall was building a sawmill on the American River. The lanky carpenter leaned over. A gleam caught his eye. Gold! Gold in California!

The Sierra Nevada was more than an awesome mountain range. Somewhere deep inside lurked the **mother lode**. Word leaked out. Within days, the rush for California gold began.

People came from Mexico, Europe, even China. But Americans had the head start. San Francisco emptied as **forty-niners** swarmed the goldfields.

CALIFORNIA
AND THE
GOLD REGION DIRECT!

The Magnificent, Fast Sailing and favorite packet Ship,

JOSEPHIN

BURTHEN 400 TONS, CAPT.

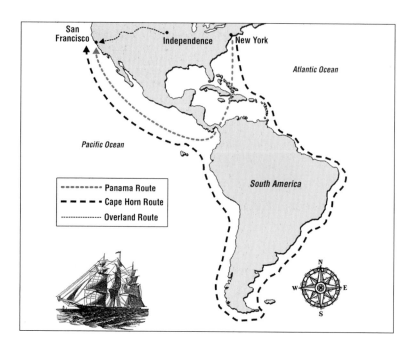

From the East, there were three routes to California. One was by boat to Panama. There people crossed the **isthmus** by coach. In Panama City, they caught another boat to San Francisco.

Some chose to sail all the way around South America. This Cape Horn route was dangerous. Even so, a number of old, undersized boats were called into service. Many fell victim to the wild, stormy seas.

Most people traveled overland. It was the cheapest way. But it was not the easiest. Many things made it difficult. There were unfriendly Indians; raging rivers; wide, waterless stretches; and looming mountains. Disease was always present. **Cholera** killed many. Still by 1852, almost 200,000 people had reached California.

Few travelers spent much time in the Great Basin. This was the land that lay east of the Sierra Nevada and west of the Rocky Mountains. That thirsty land wasn't called Nevada or Utah then. It was simply wilderness. For the most part, it was hot, dry wilderness.

A couple of snow-fed rivers ran inland, away from the sea. The ground around them was lush and fertile. Until the late 1840s, the native Indians—Paiute, Bannock, Shoshone, Goshute, and Washoe—claimed the land.

Mountain men wandered through the Great Basin. Kit Carson first explored the region in 1829. The Carson River and Carson Valley were named after him. Carson City later became the capital of Nevada. Then trailblazers like Jed Smith, Joe Walker, and John C. Fremont mapped the area in the early 1840s.

The Mormons in the Great Basin

May 1850. The Orr wagon train creaked to a stop beside the Carson River. These travelers were Mormons. They were members of the Church of Jesus Christ of Latter-day Saints. They were seeking a new life in the West.

In 1844, an angry mob in Illinois had killed the Mormon leader and prophet, Joseph Smith. The Mormons were then driven from the state.

Close to 5,000 Mormons had crossed the Great Plains and Rocky Mountains. They were searching for a place where they would be free to practice their religion.

Joseph Smith

The Mormons had settled at the eastern edge of the Great Basin. Brigham Young had became their leader. He named their new home Salt Lake City.

Young wanted to keep his church strong. So he sent some of his followers into the wilderness to establish other Mormon communities.

Brigham Young

Mormon Station, the oldest town in Nevada, nestled against the eastern foot of the Sierra Nevada. It was later named Genoa. But in the spring of 1850, Mormon Station was a Carson Valley **way station**. Many travelers heading for or from California stopped there.

The Mormons with the Orr wagon train were on their way to California. They weren't looking for gold. They just wanted lunch. And the Carson River's shady banks offered a pretty rest stop.

The men led the livestock to water. The women built cooking fires. Soon, bacon and potatoes sizzled.

One of the travelers, Bill Prouse, glanced up at the cliffs. He saw spilling rocks and a little stream. I know this place, he thought. It's called Sun Mountain. He'd found a lucky gold nugget there two years before.

Prouse grabbed a tin milk pan. He strolled over to where the stream joined the river. It was a likely spot to sift gravel. Within a few minutes, his pan sparkled. "Look!" he yelled. "Look at the gold!"

A couple of men glanced in his pan. But the others went about their business. Gold was nice if you could get it, of course. But it tempted too many people. California was swollen with prospectors. And few would get rich.

The travelers discovered that several feet of snow blanketed the Sierra Nevada passes. So the Orr wagon train couldn't go on. The **Conestogas** couldn't cross for weeks. But that wasn't such a bad thing. It had been a dry, dusty journey from Salt Lake City. Resting beside the gentle river was a blessing.

Oxen and horses grazed. Women mended and cleaned. Children ran and played. Some of the men hunted and fished. Some repaired wagons and harnesses.

Others had less to do. So why not try prospecting? They thought Prouse's stream, which he'd named Gold Creek, seemed like a good place to start.

John Orr and Nicholas Kelly worked their way upstream. On June 1, they discovered a rock formation later named Devil's Gate. Orr stuck a knife into the rock. He pried off a chunk. Behind it, a big nugget hinted at Sun Mountain's treasure.

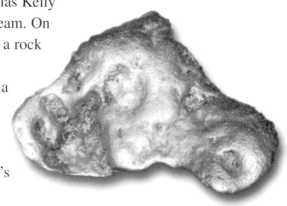

The men found a fair bit of gold. But California called. Once the snow melted, the wagons and the Mormons moved on.

But word of the Sun Mountain find quickly spread. Some 60,000 people passed the place on the way to California. A handful tried their luck up Gold Creek. One man took $30,000 in gold out of Orr's hole. Another found $8,000 worth nearby. Within a year, some 120 men prospected up Sun Mountain.

A tent town sprang up at the foot of Gold Canyon. This town was called Chinatown. It was named for the large number of Far Eastern prospectors in the area. When Nevada became a territory in 1861, the town was renamed Dayton.

On September 9, 1850, Congress created the Utah Territory. Brigham Young was appointed territorial governor.

The United States had officially adopted the Great Basin.

In 1851, a prospector named James "Old Virginny" Fennimore moved two miles up the canyon to work. Others followed. The town of Johntown was born.

Not much lumber was available. So housing was primitive. The best shelters were built of native rock. The worst shelters were crude caves dug into hillsides. These "coyote holes" worked fine in summer. But they weren't worth much once winter snow fell.

Still, the men kept working. Maybe Sun Mountain had a mother lode. But to find out, they needed tools. And they needed food for themselves and their livestock. Grazing along the Great Basin trails had turned grass to dust.

John Reese was a Mormon from Salt Lake City. One day he loaded 13 wagons with supplies. At Mormon Station, he built a store and a hotel—the only one in the area. He kept his prices high.

Other Mormons followed and settled nearby. Before long, Carson Valley's rich grassland grew excellent crops and cattle. The Mormons sold all they could raise. They also received high prices. That made the miners mad.

Chapter 2

Mucha Plata

On the other side of the Sierra Nevada, the search for gold continued. Many men were after that prize. Pickings were slim. Those with enough **seed money** opened stores. Others turned to farming, ranching, and even wine making. Many went home. But a few headed east to Sun Mountain.

Ethan and Hosea Grosh wandered east. The brothers were as big as oxen and as strong as mules. Nobody really knew the brothers well. The Groshes usually kept to themselves.

Both brothers had studied **chemistry** and **mineralogy**. No doubt they smiled when others complained about "that dang blue clay" and how it clogged their rockers.

Early prospectors used rockers. They looked like babies' cradles with one end removed. Gravel went in. Water washed through. The heavy gold fell into cleats nailed across the bottom. Everything else was thrown away.

The method worked, but not very well. Much gold was thrown away with the dirt. For every dollar made, the miners threw away two. Mounds of gold-studded blue stuff piled up.

One day, a Mexican miner happened through. The blue dirt caught his eye. "*Mucha plata!*" he shouted. "*Mucha plata!*"

Everyone thought he meant "More gold!" So they nodded and answered, "Yes, more gold."

But what he said was "Much silver!"

On November 3, 1856, the Grosh brothers wrote their father. "We have found two veins of silver at the forks of Gold Canyon. One is a perfect monster. . . ."

Sun Mountain: The Perfect Monster

Seismic activity had created the "perfect monster" thousands of years before. Earthquakes made Sun Mountain. Tremors cracked it. Precious ores filled those cracks. Some cracks had more gold. Others had more silver. The biggest deposits were great ledges of silver, buried by gold-laced gravel.

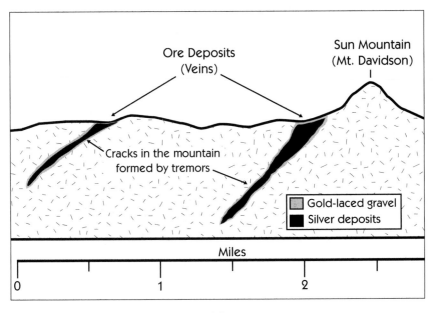

Ore Deposits (Veins)

Sun Mountain (Mt. Davidson)

Cracks in the mountain formed by tremors

Gold-laced gravel
Silver deposits

Miles

0   1   2

That gravel was what washed down the Gold and Six Mile Canyons, a few miles north. Between these two canyons stretched the divide. Beneath the divide, Sun Mountain's lode waited. It was 5 miles wide and 1,700 hundred feet deep. But it was silver, not gold.

And only the Groshes knew.

They built a stout stone cabin. Bunk beds took up one corner. **Assaying** equipment sat in another. The brothers used the equipment to test ore. Some ore was very rich in silver—as much as $3,500 per ton.

Extracting silver from rock wasn't easy. Ethan and Hosea needed special machinery. But it was expensive. And they didn't have much money.

In June of 1857, the Groshes sent ore samples to investor George Brown. He agreed to give the brothers a loan. But first, he wanted to see the veins.

By then, the brothers had found two more veins. They thought that Sun Mountain's perfect monster would make all three of them rich!

But it didn't happen that way.

Stamping machinery used to extract silver from rock

14

The End of a Dream

George Brown was on his way to Sun Mountain in September 1857. Robbers killed him and took the $600 he'd brought to invest.

Then Hosea stuck a **pick** through his foot. It wasn't a major wound. But infection set in. Sun Mountain had no doctor or wonder drugs. **Tetanus** killed Hosea soon after he heard the news of Brown's murder.

The two deaths crushed Ethan. He borrowed $60 and gave Hosea the finest funeral Sun Mountain had ever seen. Then he packed his belongings. Winter was closing in. He'd spend it working the California **placers**. By spring, he'd have the money he needed.

Ethan needed someone to watch the cabin. So before he left, Ethan struck a deal with "Old Pancake." Henry Comstock had earned that nickname because he ate pancakes morning, noon, and night. He was a drunk and a **braggart**. He was lazy to the core. He had one pink eye that turned red when he yelled. And that was often.

But Old Pancake had always believed in Sun Mountain's treasure. He lacked ambition. But he wasn't a fool. He had figured the Groshes knew more than they'd let on. For one thing, they kept getting packages, books, beakers, and chemicals.

One night before Hosea died, Old Pancake had peeked in the Groshes' window. He had watched the brothers cooking that dang blue sand. Cooking sand! What did it mean? He meant to find out.

So when Ethan asked him to keep an eye on the cabin, Old Pancake agreed. Ethan promised him a quarter of the Grosh claim. But he didn't mention where—or what—it was.

In November 1857, Ethan and his friend Dick Bucke set out across the Sierra Nevada. A favorite mule carried food, ammunition, maps, and ore samples.

In good weather, the trip to Sacramento took three days. And the sky looked clear when the two men started. But near Bigler Lake (Tahoe), a blizzard hit. The wind howled. The snow drifted. The men and the mule stumbled into Squaw Valley.

They couldn't go on. They couldn't turn around. So they rode out the storm the best they could.

Then their food gave out. They had no choice but to eat the mule. Their matches and powder got wet. No ammo, no fire. The men were in trouble!

After several days, they were rescued. Both men had severe frostbite. Bucke survived, minus one leg and his other foot. Ethan wasn't so lucky. Sun Mountain's secret was buried with him.

Back at the cabin, Old Pancake grew restless. He poured over the Grosh brothers' papers. But he couldn't make heads nor tails out of their scrawls. Finally, news of Ethan's death reached Old Pancake.

He'd never know the secret! In a rage, Comstock put a match to the brothers' cursed **scribblings**. He burned them all.

Old Pancake took off on his one-eyed, swaybacked horse. Sun Mountain's treasure belonged to him. And he'd get it one way or another.

Chapter 3

Misfits, Miners, and Miss Eilley

Comstock's Lode

Men like Henry "Old Pancake" Comstock and James "Old Virginny" Fennimore were misfits. They didn't have families. They didn't keep friends. Oh, they'd hang out with other prospectors. They'd have a few drinks and swap stories. Sometimes they'd even dance with one another. Women were scarce on Sun Mountain in the early days.

Eilley Orrum was one of the few women who came and stayed. At 15, this Scottish lass had married a Mormon and come west. Once in Salt Lake City, Eilley's husband took a second wife. Eilley wanted no part of that. So she moved on.

In Johntown, she built a big log cabin. The pretty young woman took in boarders and fed hungry miners her famous pork and beans. Eilley's became *the* place to gather. Visitors would sit before the fire and maybe even puff on a cigar.

Her home also served as the post office when Snowshoe Thompson arrived from California. He was the mountain mailman.

A visit from Snowshoe Thompson brought everyone running. Letters from home! Packages wrapped in twine! Inside were treasures like eyeglasses and socks. The scruffy men would clap and holler like little kids. Of course, the Johntowners whooped it up whenever it seemed proper.

On Washington's birthday in 1858, Old Virginny rode up to Eilley's. "Hey, fellers," he called. "Just come across a likely ledge. Staked me a claim too."

Sure enough, tucked under a rock, a piece of paper said "James Fennimore, February 22, 1858."

Henry Comstock was not happy when he heard the news. Early the next morning, he rode into the hills. He staked claims everywhere—trees, rocks, logs, boulders. Sun Mountain was wallpapered with "Comstock." Then he stood atop Devil's Gate. He shouted to all passersby, "Halt! This is Comstock's Lode!"

And so it got its name.

By the end of 1858, the gravel in the lower canyons didn't hold much gold. Everyone aimed uphill. They were looking for something richer. And work continued despite the first snows.

January 1859. Shouts of joy sent Old Pancake slipping down an icy hill. He found four men. One of them was Old Virginny. Gold shimmered brightly in their pans.

"Claim jumpers!" shouted Comstock.

The four only laughed and kept on washing the gold. "Just because you put your name on every rock on this here mountain! That don't mean you own the place!"

18

The men didn't know it, but they'd found the southern outcroppings of the Comstock Lode. For luck, they called the place Gold Hill. It would become the site of the Yellow Jacket and Crown Point mines.

By spring, every Johntowner had moved to Gold Hill. Eilley Orrum moved too—log cabin and all. The men stretched out along the divide, still hunting gold.

In June, Pete O'Reilly and Pat McLaughlin were digging a spring near the head of Six Mile Canyon. It took water to wash gravel away from the gold. Atop Sun Mountain, that precious liquid was in short supply. As they dug, they noticed how the sand sparkled.

Old Pancake rode up just then. "Congratulations, boys. You've found yourselves some gold, all right. Just one little problem. That there water belongs to me and my business partners."

Manny Penrod, Old Virginny, and Old Pancake had bought the water rights above Six Mile Canyon the year before.

The Irishmen turned green as shamrocks. They needed that water to get at the gold.

"Tell ya what," offered Comstock. "Give me 100 feet of your claim. Then you can have the water."

19

The duo signed a paper to make it legal. Old Pancake was a lucky man. The site became the Ophir Mine. It was the first big strike on the Comstock Lode.

Comstock hurried off to square things with Manny Penrod. He'd deal with Old Virginny later. He would never forgive that claim jumper!

Rumor had it no one could beat James Fennimore at prospecting. At least no one could beat him when he was sober. But that wasn't often.

That night, Comstock found Old Virginny well on his way to drunk. Old Pancake opened another bottle. About dawn, he walked off with Fennimore's share of the Six Mile Canyon site. The price was one half blind, swaybacked horse and a bottle of wine. Those 33 feet of the Ophir were soon worth $60,000.

Then people joked, "Old Virginny has a $60,000 horse. But he can't afford a saddle to ride it."

Civilization moved up from Gold Hill, across the divide, toward the Ophir. A city of tents, 100 strong, draped the steep slope. Twice that many coyote holes dotted the mountain.

Ten saloons satisfied thirsty miners. One night, Old Virginny stumbled out of one, tripped, and fell. His whiskey bottle crashed against the ground. Turning his face toward the moon, Fennimore shouted, "I christen this place Virginia Town."

The name stuck.

Nevada Silver

On both ends of the mountain, work continued. The diggings looked promising at first. The veins of gold were wide. But about ten feet deep, the gold turned blue. Not one miner suspected silver.

One cattle rancher did. He was B. A. Harrison. The rancher showed an ore sample to his friend Judge Walsh. The judge had it tested. Assayer Melville Atwood couldn't believe it. The blue stuff was almost pure silver. "Per ton, it's worth $3,200 in silver, $1,500 in gold," Atwood claimed.

Walsh's jaw dropped. "Swear not to tell a soul!"

"What's in it for me?" asked Atwood.

The judge thought a minute. "Two hundred feet of claim."

"I swear," Atwood promised.

Walsh headed straight for Virginia City. His saddlebags bulged with money. By hook or by crook, he would buy up the Comstock Lode before its secret leaked out.

Walsh didn't have much of a head start. Atwood just couldn't keep quiet. News spread quickly—clear to San Francisco. The California placers had shrunk. Now they only yielded pocket change. And the promise of Nevada silver beckoned.

Back in Virginia City, the miners still didn't have a clue. With the gold mostly gone, they were ready to sell. Comstock had already traded part of his claim for two mules. Those mules cost him $6 million.

Manny Penrod sold out for $8,500. Pat McLaughlin took $2,500 from George Hearst. This San Franciscan arrived a few days after Walsh. He became the first Comstock Lode millionaire.

To celebrate, George Hearst bought his son, William, a newspaper. That newspaper became the *San Francisco Examiner* and was the start of the Hearst empire. McLaughlin died broke.

William Hearst

Old Pancake held out as long as he could. Finally, he sold the rest of his claim to Walsh for $11,000. Comstock opened a dry goods store in the Carson Valley. But he wasn't much of a businessman. He soon lost everything.

Pete O'Reilly's final price tag was $445,000. Then he gambled it away.

And those were the misfortunes of the original Sun Mountain settlers. There were two exceptions—Eilley Orrum and Lemuel "Sandy" Bowers. They had a large number of mine **stocks**.

Along the way, several miners had traded claim shares for Eilley's room and board.

She hung on to every one. One of her boarders was Sandy Bowers. When Eilley and Sandy got married, so did their shares. Combined the shares brought in $250,000 per year.

Eilley wasn't finished. "We'll build a **stamp mill**."

To separate silver from ore, the rock needed to be crushed, or stamped. The mill they built had 24 stamps. It could crush 20 tons of ore each day. At $100 per ton, the Bowers made another $1 million per year.

"We've got money to throw at the birds," noted Sandy Bowers. The couple built a mansion and traveled around Europe for several years.

Chapter 4

Seekers, Soldiers, and Chief Winnemucca

Crossing the Sierra Nevada

November 22, 1859. Early snowfall halted the surge of silver seekers. Most stopped at Hangtown (Placerville), California. They were afraid of getting stranded in the Sierra Nevada. A few struggled farther. They wanted to be first across the mountains come spring.

No one dared challenge the 50-foot snowdrifts that blocked the passes now. The winter of '59 was one to reckon with.

By December, things were bleak in Virginia City. Thousands of stove pipes dotted the hills. But fuel was scarce. Only a few stunted trees and sagebrush could be found. Cutting those meant hiking farther and farther through waist-deep snow. The hillsides were bare before spring.

Livestock could not survive such weather. According to Dan DeQuille, editor of Virginia City's *Territorial Enterprise*, "Not only cattle but horses, donkeys, and animals of all kinds died of cold and hunger. Most of them starved to death."

No humans starved. But plenty went hungry. Supplies couldn't get in. Flour sold for $75 per 100-pound sack. If that wasn't bad enough, the saloons ran completely out of liquor.

There were avalanches too. And when the weather warmed in February, flash floods came. The "Washoe **zephyr**" visited regularly. The Washoe zephyr became a wicked wind. It blew over the Sierra Nevada, picking up speed. Crossing the Carson Valley, it hit with gale force. When it rammed Sun Mountain, canvas tents and houses flew everywhere.

But the miners waited through it all. Finally, warm March temperatures arrived. The miners headed for Virginia City. The trail was narrow, choked, and muddy. If one wagon got stuck, so did those behind it.

In good conditions, crossing the Sierra Nevada took three days. In the spring of 1860, it took weeks.

John Moore left San Francisco on March 9. Loaded with blankets, tin plates, and assorted liquors, his wagon made its way to Sun Mountain in 22 days.

Upon arrival, he put up a tent and laid carpet right on the dirt. Then he ripped a board from his wagon and built a bar. Moore's Saloon and Boardinghouse was officially open. Within hours, he had sold $200 in beverages and had rented 32 blankets to sleepy miners. Not beds, just blankets! For an extra 50 cents, miners could have a pillowcase stuffed with straw.

By summer, some 10,000 silver seekers made their way to Virginia City. It was a rough-and-tumble town. Fistfights and bullets settled arguments. And there was plenty to argue about.

Duels, Lawsuits, and the Civil War

The early mining claims proved questionable. They were recorded in pencil in a journal that was kept in a saloon. Anyone could have a look—or erase something!

The original claims were for ownership of the surface ground. But the Comstock Lode's silver veins went deep. They dipped, angled, and curved. Many times, they overlapped. That made it hard to say exactly who owned what.

Eventually, lawsuits replaced **duels**. Attorney William Stewart had a reputation for honesty and a head for mining law. He landed in Virginia City early in 1860. Within five years, he had made $1 million.

Bringing law to a lawless land wasn't easy. A single United States marshal tried to keep the peace. But judges were often **bought**. And juries were bribed. There was no government to speak of. That is unless you counted the territorial government in Salt Lake City. And few people in Virginia City wanted anything to do with Mormon law.

Bigger battles brewed. In the East, the Civil War loomed. The territories, Utah included, could upset the balance of power between North and South. Would they be free or slave?

Judge David Terry was a **secessionist** from California. He came to Virginia City with one goal. He wanted to claim the Comstock Lode for the South. The Confederacy needed her silver. Terry led a band of Southern sympathizers. Each carried a weapon where everyone could see it.

Judge David Terry

25

The Rebel militia built a series of stone forts along the divide. Meanwhile, Terry talked up slavery. Many people listened. And they agreed. Slaves would provide cheap labor.

But most people in Virginia City stood behind Bill Stewart. He was an outspoken **abolitionist**. The 100-member fire department supported him. Many had served as New York City firemen. All were big, brave Northerners.

The mine owners rallied against David Terry too. He was on their land! Why did he think he could just waltz in and take control?

So the two sides gathered forces and waited for America to go to war.

The Paiute War

May 8, 1860. A Pony Express rider thundered up Sun Mountain. "The Paiutes are on the warpath!"

Indians had burned Williams Station to the ground. All five men inside died.

The news shocked Virginia City and nearby towns. Chief  Winnemucca's tribe had never given the settlers any trouble before. But if they wanted trouble, well . . .

Under Major Ormsby, 105 volunteers marched down the Carson River. The men headed for Pyramid Lake, Chief Winnemucca's stomping grounds. The ragtag crew was poorly armed and most did not have horses. But the volunteers figured the Paiutes would turn tail and run.

Chief Winnemucca

26

A few miles away, a small band of Paiutes approached. One waved a white flag. But peace was not on the townspeople's minds. Someone opened fire.

The Indians retreated up a ravine. The white men followed. Suddenly, 200 Paiutes surrounded them. Shots rang out. Men and horses fell. Major Ormsby was among them. Of the 105 volunteers, only 29 escaped.

People in Virginia City panicked. Rumors ran wild. Had 5,000 Paiutes gathered? Would they attack Virginia City? Many people headed for California. Others stood their ground.

"There were but two classes of persons in the place," wrote DeQuille. "Those who were not at all frightened and those who were frightened almost out of their wits."

The call for troops went out to California. The Sierra Battalion marched over the mountains. Captain Edward Storey organized the 1,000 Volunteer Virginia Rifles. When the United States infantry arrived, the forces set out for Pyramid Lake.

Pyramid Lake

It was a short battle. The Paiutes lost 160 men. Many more were wounded. Only two white men died. One of them was Captain Storey. In his honor, the land surrounding Virginia City became Storey County.

After the captain's funeral, the Sierra Battalion broke camp. Their commander, Colonel Hayes, needed a place to store extra weapons and ammunition. Since there was no **arsenal** in the region, he needed a secure location. And he needed someone responsible to be in charge of the weapons.

Hayes met with Judge Terry. The judge promised to keep the weapons safe in his fort above Gold Hill. Then the California force went home. They didn't realize that they had just armed Virginia City's Confederates.

Three months later, Chief Winnemucca came to call. He explained that his people had always wanted to live in peace with the white men. In fact, they had never killed the men at Williams Station.

Bannock Indians were responsible. They'd had good reason. The murdered men had kidnapped the Bannocks' women and held them prisoner. Some Shoshone had joined the Bannock Indians in their quest for vengeance. There were also a few "bad" Paiutes. But no one was from the chief's tribe.

The old chief shook his head. Too bad the white men shot first and asked questions later. He only hoped that the current peace would last.

With the Paiute War behind them, the Virginians' thoughts once again turned to silver.

Chapter 5

Outlaws, Walking Rocks, and Mark Twain

Sun Mountain's silver was a magnet. Eager investors bought stock in Virginia City. Everyone wanted Comstock Lode shares. Their money built mines and roads. Churches, stores, and fine hotels followed. It seemed that Virginia City had grown up overnight.

Stacked streets **terraced** the hillside. Different levels represented different layers of society. Uphill, pretty houses with balconies overlooked A and B streets. Hotels, stores, and banks lined C Street. D Street belonged to the working class.

Below that on E Street was Chinatown. A certain amount of **prejudice** fell on the Chinese. The mines never hired them. Those jobs were saved for white people. So in the late 1860s, Chinese laborers helped build the Virginia & Truckee Railroad (V&T). They also did laundry and mending for many of the townspeople.

At the bottom level, just above the city dump, lived the native people. The "always hungry" Paiutes lived as best they could. Many collected firewood. Then they sold six-stick bundles for $1.

Ophir Company v. McCall

Between 1859 and 1864, some 28 mines were dug in the Comstock Lode. Besides the Ophir, several produced rich ore. They included the Gould & Curry and the Chollar-Potosi (1861); the Yellow Jacket, the Belcher, and the Savage (1863); and the Crown Point (1864).

As usual, claims often overlapped. To settle the disputes, the owners turned to Bill Stewart. The attorney hired **geologists**,

The Ophir Mine

surveyors, and **engineers**. At last, boundary lines were legally drawn.

The owners joined forces again to fight Judge Terry. As before, they went to Stewart. North and South went head to head. But they didn't meet on a battlefield. They met in a courtroom. The winner of *Ophir Company v. McCall* would control the Comstock Lode. But neither side won a clear victory.

McCall had **squatted** on land claimed by the Ophir. Judge David Terry defended him. Bill Stewart represented the mine. Stewart proved his case better. But the trial ended in a **hung** jury. Eight jurors voted for the Ophir. Four voted for McCall. Those four worked for Terry. They were part of a **gang** known as the "Rich Company." These men served Judge Terry any way they could—usually by breaking the law.

Since there was no judgment, the gang figured crime just might pay. Armed with Sierra Battalion rifles, they took to robbing freight wagons and stages.

One day, the thugs walked right into the St. Louis Company Mine. Pointing guns at the owners, the gang told them to leave. "This claim now belongs to the Confederacy." Some thought the Civil War might start right there.

Instead, Stewart took Terry back to court. This time he won. Terry was enough of a "Southern gentleman" to take the defeat in stride. A heavily armed posse chased the Rich Company off Sun Mountain.

Except for some saloon brawls, the Civil War was over in Nevada. (Nevada broke off from Utah in 1861 to become a separate territory.)

Later, Nevada would play an important role in the War Between the States. Abraham Lincoln needed Northern votes in Congress. The Nevada Territory was rich in mineral wealth and clearly pro-Union. Lincoln pushed for statehood.

Nevada became a state on October 31, 1864. Her vote for the Thirteenth Amendment abolished slavery in America.

Samuel Clemens Comes to Nevada

Meanwhile, the Nevada Territory needed representation in government. James Nye was appointed governor in 1861. He named Orion Clemens the territorial secretary.

Clemens' brother, Samuel, had just quit his job as a riverboat pilot. Fighting for the Confederacy didn't seem like a good plan to him. But a trip out West sounded exciting. He and Orion climbed aboard a stagecoach. Twenty bumpy days later, they arrived in Nevada.

Orion went to work. But Sam went exploring.

Samuel ended up at Lake Tahoe. There he and a couple of buddies staked a timber claim.

But no one wanted to cut logs. The place was too pretty. Besides the fishing was awesome. A boat trip on the crystal clear water was like a "balloon voyage." The three spent days just floating around. Clemens called the lake "the fairest picture the whole earth affords."

They might have stayed there forever. But one night after a drink or two, young Sam set the forest on fire. The trio retreated in a hurry. Sam moved on to Aurora. He was ready to try his hand at gold mining.

About that time, the *Territorial Enterprise* received some stories in the mail. "Josh," the author, had a witty, honest style. He was offered a job. Samuel "Josh" Clemens arrived in Virginia City and changed his pen name to "Mark Twain."

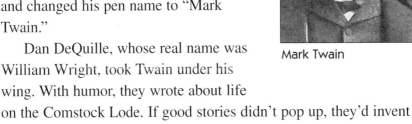

Mark Twain

Dan DeQuille, whose real name was William Wright, took Twain under his wing. With humor, they wrote about life on the Comstock Lode. If good stories didn't pop up, they'd invent tall tales.

DeQuille wrote about magnetic stones that "walked" under their own power. He also reported on a **fictional** ice helmet that supposedly made crossing the desert easier. Its inventor, according to DeQuille, froze to death in the middle of the wilderness. Rescuers found him with icicles hanging from his body. Apparently, DeQuille wrote, the helmet had a defect.

People in Virginia City found the tall tales amusing. The rest of the world believed them. Many newspapers ran stories about the helmet inventor's untimely death. German scientists wrote to "Dr. DeQuille" to learn more about his magic rocks. Even P. T. Barnum, of circus fame, wanted to show the rocks under his big top.

P. T. Barnum

Life in Virginia City

By 1863, over 15,000 people called Virginia City home. There were families, a school for the children, and two churches. A new bank made loans and handled the large sums of money provided by the mines.

Entertainers performed in Maguire's Opera House. It had a stable in the basement. Odd odors drifted up through the floorboards. But no one complained. Smelly entertainment was better than none at all. Eventually, Piper's Opera House replaced Maguire's. "Big-name" entertainers included Edwin Booth, brother of John Wilkes Booth, and Lotta Crabtree.

Supply wagons drawn by 16-mule teams crowded the streets. Animal lameness, accidents, and driver error caused regular traffic jams. These happened almost every day. Often, the jams lasted for hours.

Six stagecoach lines serviced Virginia City. DeQuille wrote that the coaches arrived loaded with "**capitalists**, miners, thieves, robbers, and adventurers of all kinds."

The coaches were robbed regularly. Both Wells Fargo **strongboxes** and passengers lost their valuables.

One particularly clever gang lived in Six Mile Canyon. Everyone thought they were miners. After all, the mill they'd leased was "producing" silver bars. Nobody suspected those bars had been raided from the stages.

But the Six Mile gang got greedy. They robbed a Central Pacific train, taking $41,000. The railroad put its best detectives to work. The thieves were soon behind *iron bars*.

Sun Mountain had other dangers. Tunnels and mine shafts were everywhere. A number of people, not to mention animals, fell into them. Some were rescued. Some simply vanished.

As ore was removed, the ground became unstable. Sinkholes swallowed wagons, livestock—even buildings.

On August 29, 1863, fire swept through Virginia City. The blaze started in a carpenter's shop. Over 2,000 people were left homeless. More property might have been saved.

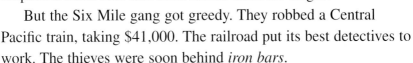

But two of the town's four fire departments got into a fight. Both wanted to be first on the scene. Neither was. So instead, the blaze spun out of control.

Such was life in young Virginia City.

Chapter 6

Wooden Skyscrapers

Cave-Ins

The Comstock Lode was indeed a monster. The silver veins plunged down into the heart of Sun Mountain. As the "easy" surface ore was removed, the mines carved ever deeper. The veins showed no signs of stopping. In fact, they grew even wider. This led to new problems.

Early on, buckets carried men down into the earth and lifted the ore out. The first round shafts looked like water wells. They were up to 50 feet deep. Then square, timber-supported shafts replaced the round ones.

By December 1860, the Ophir was 180 feet deep. There, in the "third **gallery**," the vein was 45 feet wide. No one knew how to safely remove such a width of ore. If the miners dug out the whole vein, the ground above would collapse. The usual supports just wouldn't work.

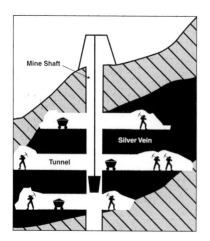

Mine Shaft

Silver Vein

Tunnel

First, the timbers weren't long enough. The nearby trees were stunted. Few grew over 20 feet tall. Bolting two together to create a longer timber made the support weak. So there was no safe way to work above or below the supports. Removing ore from either end loosened the timbers. Cave-ins were the often fatal results.

The Ophir's owners sent for Philip Deidesheimer. The German engineer had been mining in California. Within three weeks, he had an idea. His "square set" method worked perfectly.

Timbers were framed into rectangles. These five-foot by six-foot "cribs" could be stacked as high as necessary. As they piled on top of one another, they were filled with waste rock. The stone pillars could support a great deal of weight.

No one ever came up with a better design. Unfortunately, Deidesheimer never bothered to patent his invention. If he had, he would have become a wealthy man. Instead, he died in poverty.

Timber for the Mines

Next came the question of where to find the timber. The nearby hillsides had already been stripped. The lowlands below faced a similar fate. It didn't take long to cut every tree in the Washoe and Carson Valleys.

Lumberjacks started up the eastern Sierra Nevada. Soon they reached the forests surrounding Lake Tahoe. During the 1860s, countless trees fell.

DeQuille put it bluntly. "The Comstock Lode may truthfully be said to be the tomb of the forests of the Sierras. Millions on millions of feet of lumber are **annually** buried in the mines."

Lumberjacks **clear-cut** their way around Lake Tahoe. Hundred-foot firs and sugar pines fell victim.

At waterfront mills, the logs were gathered into large rafts. Small steamboats towed them to the eastern shore. Then out of the water and onto the track they went. A railroad tugged them to the top of the mountain. Then their ride really began!

The huge logs were loaded into a V-shaped trough filled with running water. This giant **flume** whisked the timber 20 miles down the eastern slope. At the bottom, *splash!* They crashed into holding ponds. From there, wagons hauled them up Sun Mountain, bound for burial. In later years, the V&T Railroad hauled the logs.

Underground Cities

Picture how a big mine looked. Up to 1,000 men might be working underground at one time. DeQuille explained that such an operation was "a considerable village, though it be a village far below the light of day."

It was more like a **subterranean** city, complete with wooden skyscrapers. Stacked cribs rose as high as 2,000 feet. Countless staircases led from floor to floor. Chutes and **winzes** connected them as well. Heavy plank "sidewalks" carried workers on every level. And as the miners chiseled away at the Comstock Lode, the underground cities grew.

Milling the Silver

Once the ore came out of the ground, it had to be milled. Before 1860, the richest ore was shipped to England. It was an expensive way to go. But the British process extracted 90 percent of the silver, or $1,000 per ton.

Lower-grade ore stayed on Sun Mountain, waiting for local mills to be built. The first mill, the Pioneer, was constructed at Devil's Gate. Others followed. At first, the mills sat on top of Sun Mountain.

The millers continually worked to figure out the best way to extract silver. "All manner of experiments were tried," wrote DeQuille. He compared the mixing pans to witches' cauldrons.

The crushed rock was combined with a number of things. The millers were looking for something that would bond with the silver. They tried minerals, such as borax, alum, potash, and saltpeter.

"Not satisfied," joked DeQuille, "they went to the hills and started in on the vegetable kingdom." Various plants and barks were boiled into strong teas. Sagebrush was bitter and abundant and was a favorite. Millers hoped a tea bath would scrub silver from rock.

After two years, they settled on the "Washoe pan process." The ore was stamped and mixed with water. This **slurry** was put into big vats with quicksilver (mercury), salt, and copper sulfate.

Steam heat forced the silver to bond with the mercury. The slurry then traveled through a series of settling basins. This separated the **amalgam**

Ruins of a stamping mill

from the rock. The leftovers were called *tailings*.

The process required a lot of water. Mills were built along the Carson River and Washoe Lake. At the downhill mills, the mercury-tainted tailings were dumped on site. The uphill mills tossed them into the canyons. Or they hauled the waste below for disposal.

Spring snowmelt and rain washed the tailings into the river, streams, and lake. They've spread out over time. But they haven't gone away.

For many years, no one thought to collect them. Too bad. Those tailings held millions in silver and gold. And mercury isn't the healthiest thing to have in rivers.

Finally, someone decided to save the tailings. They were worked and reworked in several ways. Large amounts of precious metals were **reclaimed**. But no amount of work could remove every trace.

Steam Inside the Mountain

Meanwhile, Sun Mountain had new surprises. You might think the inside of a mountain is a cool, dry place. But the deeper the miners went, the hotter it got. And the wetter it became.

Along with clay and silver, the ore contained **porphyry**, a really strange rock studded with little crystals. When it comes into contact with oxygen, porphyry swells. It's sort of like bread soaking up moisture.

As the porphyry expanded, water seeped around it. With the heat, the leaking water steamed. That made it even hotter, making yet more steam. It wasn't a great environment. The men got cramps, headaches, and nausea. If they **ascended** too quickly, they got the **bends**. This is the same condition that affects deep-sea divers when they surface too quickly.

Sometimes miners had to come up in a hurry. Pockets of poisonous gas hid behind thin rock walls.

One wrong chip of the ax could make a man sick for days. One wrong push of the shovel might drown the guy.

On top of the mountain, water was in short supply. Inside the mountain, a guy could find plenty. But it was hot, foul water. And there was no shortage of it. Flooded shafts halted many operations. Small, hastily dug tunnels drained some of the water. But it kept creeping back.

The newspapers called for a more permanent solution. Like a *really big* tunnel. A German immigrant answered the call.

Chapter 7

The War of the Silver Kings

Adolph Sutro

Adolph Sutro had ridden the 1849 rush to California. There, he made his first fortune. It wasn't in gold, but in dry goods and real estate.

In 1860, Sutro took a trip to the Comstock Lode. Immediately, he saw the need for a railroad to haul ore. He agreed that a deep tunnel would increase airflow and drainage to the mines. But both would be years away.

Adolph Sutro

A more immediate problem captured his attention. What *was* the best way to extract silver and gold from the ore? Sutro sold his California holdings and built a mill on the Carson River. Within three years, his Dayton operation saw a profit of $10,000 per month.

But an 1863 fire burned the mill to the ground. Insurance money in hand, Sutro looked for something to do. The tunnel project, called "impossible" by many, fit the bill. He hired geologist Baron von Richtofen to study the proper route.

Surveys in hand, Sutro went to the Nevada state legislature. In 1865, he was given a **franchise** to dig his tunnel.

A year later, the United States Congress passed the Sutro Tunnel Act. That gave Sutro title to the land and the right to charge for the tunnel's use. Now all he needed was $3 million to build it. He went east to seek financing.

The Depression

At the time, Virginia City was smack in the middle of a **depression**. By 1865, the mines had reached 500 feet. There in the fourth gallery, the ore seemed to give out. Fifty working mines shut down. Their total value fell from $40 million to $4 million.

The price of mining stocks tumbled. Large and small investors lost everything. Some 10,000 people were out of work. Many packed up and moved on.

A handful saw opportunity. It's been said that Nevada silver built San Francisco. Construction began when the silver kings went to war.

William Sharon was a San Francisco banker. In 1864, he founded the Bank of California with William Ralston and Darius O. Mills. The Virginia City branch opened in November.

Virginia City needed money. Despite the depression, Sharon loaned it. A lot of it. He charged two percent interest, which was well below the going rate. When the price of mining stock crashed in 1865, many businesses couldn't make their payments. Every time the bank **foreclosed**, the bank's assets grew.

The Comeback

When Baron von Richtofen surveyed Sun Mountain, he'd gone down into the mines and studied the veins. He believed they did not **play out** at 500 feet. Rather, he felt they dipped to the east and reached greater depths than ever imagined.

He released his report some time in 1865. No one knows when his findings became common knowledge. But William Sharon had an inside track. So quietly, he gained control of many mills and mines for pennies on the dollar. These included the Yellow Jacket and the Chollar-Potosi.

Sharon, Ralston, and Mills formed the Union Mill & Mining Company. By 1869, "Ralston's Ring" owned all the biggest mines and 17 mills.

Smaller claims could also be had cheap. A little mine called the Kentuck proved a windfall for John Mackay and J. M. Walker.

Mackay Hits Pay Dirt

John Mackay was an experienced miner when he hit Virginia City. He and Jack O'Brien wandered over from California in 1860. Legend tells of their arrival.

> The two topped the last rise. Spotting
> Virginia City, O'Brien turned to Mackay.
> "Have you any money?" he asked.
> "Not a red cent." Mackay answered.
> O'Brien reached into his pocket. He tossed
> his last half-dollar into the brush. "Now
> we'll walk into camp like gentlemen."

Later, Mackay neither confirmed nor denied the story. But he admitted, "That's what Jack did with all his money." This is probably why Mackay ended their partnership.

John Mackay

Mackay found a job as a mine laborer. The $4 pay per day wasn't bad. In fact, no mining district in the world could match it.

Comstock Lode miners organized a union. Besides higher wages, they worked shorter hours. With the heat and **ventilation** problems, six-hour workdays were common.

But Mackay had bigger dreams. Within a year, he'd become an independent contractor. He specialized in building square-set cribs. With every paycheck, he bought Comstock Lode shares. By 1863, he owned stock in four small mines.

Two years later, he and Walker became partners in management of the Bullion mine. That venture failed. But the men learned a valuable lesson. Too many stockholders could spoil a good thing. When they bought the Kentuck, they kept the operation small. And they didn't sell stock.

The Kentuck struck silver in 1866. Mackay made his first million. Walker sold out for $600,000. Between 1866 and 1869, the mine produced almost $4 million.

William Sharon hit the roof! How had he let the Kentuck slip through his fingers?

Jim Fair

Mackay teamed with fellow Irishman Jim Fair. Fair was also an accomplished miner. But unlike Mackay, he was not a "people person." He was into machines. So when he perfected a "better" milling process, he brought it to the Comstock Lode.

45

He and Mackay hatched a plan to take control of another mine, Hale & Norcross. At the time, it belonged to the Bank of California. With no ore showing, the price of the stock hit bottom.

So Fair and Mackay started to buy cheap Hale & Norcross shares. By March 1869, Fair, Mackay, and two business partners owned controlling interest in the mine. They hit pay dirt later that year.

Tunnel or Railroad?

Meanwhile, Sutro had returned to Virginia City. He'd raised some money to build a tunnel. But he needed more financing. He thought that since the mining companies would benefit from the tunnel, they would surely chip in.

Ralston's Ring had other plans. They already owned most of the mines and mills. If they built a railroad to carry ore between the mines and the mills, they'd have a Comstock Lode **monopoly**. Sharon led the fight against the tunnel. Sutro's dream looked ready to go up in smoke. Instead, a terrible fire gave him all the ammunition he needed.

On April 7, 1869, at 4 a.m., the Yellow Jacket night shift finished. But someone left a candle burning against a bone-dry timber. Three hours later, the day shift arrived. They found the mine in flames—800 feet below ground!

The men turned to run. Burning timbers fell. Boom! An explosion followed. The miners heard "a wind like a gale." *Whoosh!* Fire, fumes, and smoke blew into two connected mines, the Kentuck and the Crown Point.

Whistles blew. Alarms sounded. The fire companies were quick to the scene. But fighting a blaze so deep underground was impossible. All thoughts turned to getting the men out alive.

The cages went up and down, as quickly as they could. Finally, no more signals came from below. At morning's end, 37 men had died.

The fire kept burning. All three shafts were sealed. Water and steam were pumped in. It took six months for the charred wooden city to stop smoldering.

Sutro went to the Miners' Union. With drawings and charts, he showed them exactly how his tunnel could have saved the trapped miners. He left with $50,000. That was enough to start construction. The project took seven years to complete.

Tunnel or no tunnel, the Bank of California built its railroad. The V&T was steep and crooked. The track snaked $13^{1}/2$ miles down Sun Mountain. It dropped 116 feet every mile. It tunneled through hillsides and spanned wide ravines.

In Carson City, the V&T turned north to Reno. There, it connected with the Central Pacific. From survey to completion, it took only nine months to build the railroad. Ralston's Ring had won that battle.

But the following year, they lost the war.

Chapter 8

The Big Bonanza

The year was 1870—year of *borrasca*. The Spanish word meant "poor weather." In Virginia City, it meant "lean times."

Silver production dropped off. More mines suffered hot-water floods. Stock prices again tumbled. The Crown Point mine stock fell to $2 per share. The Consolidated Virginia and Belcher mine stocks bottomed out at $1. With $3 million invested, the Bank of California grew uneasy.

But it was just another Comstock Lode tease. Out of *borrasca* again came a **bonanza**. In November, the Crown Point hit ore at 1,100 feet. The vein reached into the Belcher. William Sharon had purchased thousands of mine shares when prices had hit bottom. When stock prices hit $300 a share, his Bank of California jumped solidly back into the black.

Across town, Mackay and his partners had been busy too. The Consolidated Virginia mine had never made a profit. But Mackay believed it was a "good gamble." By January 1872, he and his partners owned 75 percent. In September, they found low-grade ore.

Mackay's men followed the vein away from the main Comstock Lode workings. The gamble paid off. Below the streets of Virginia City, some 1,200 feet deep, they found the Big Bonanza. Sun Mountain, now called Mt. Davidson, had opened her treasure chest.

Mackay and his partners became the Pacific Mill & Mining Company. They bought up the Belcher, Gould & Curry, Central, and California mines. They built mills and paid themselves for milling their own ore.

They even constructed a water pipeline. It brought Virginia City clean, tasty snowmelt. It came clear from Marlette Lake, some 20 miles away.

The Consolidated Virginia mine turned into a tourist attraction. Everyone wanted a look at the Comstock Lode's perfect monster. Bankers, politicians, preachers, even housewives traded street clothes for sturdier garb. Then down they went, into the gut of Mt. Davidson. All came away amazed by the magnificent, shimmering cavern.

In December 1874, newspaper publisher Charles de Young went below. Afterward, his San Francisco *Chronicle* raved about the Big Bonanza. Stock prices went through the roof. De Young, of course, had bought Con Virginia stock right before the boom.

The Consolidated Virginia (Con Virginia) mine

The Richest Little City in the West

That was a merry Christmas for the richest little city in the West. Everyone was making money. Elsewhere, laborers earned $1 or $2 per day. In Virginia City, miners made $4. Bootmakers made $5. Carpenters, who couldn't build houses fast enough, got $6. **Masons** took home $8, a monstrous wage at that time. Most invested a little in the stock market.

Barmaids, saloon keepers, dirt-poor prospectors, and others made fortunes. Not only did they live the American dream. They invented it!

One hundred saloons kept busy, day and night. Establishments like the Washoe Club offered private smoking and reading rooms, **billiards**, and cards. Gambling, though technically illegal, was a widespread recreation. Others preferred the theaters, which often sold out.

Restaurants served fancy meals. Fresh oysters and champagne were a favored treat. Packed in ice, the shellfish came by coach from California. How popular were they? Discarded shells piled up in the dump. The mounds remained 100 years later!

In May 1875, Mackay and his partners founded Nevada Bank. There was a small branch in Virginia City. Mackay moved to San Francisco and took over the larger San Francisco branch. He didn't care for banking. But he did enjoy the lifestyle it provided his family.

Mackay later invested in steamships, an early New York subway, and **transatlantic** telegraph cables. He died in 1902. John Mackay, who came to Virginia flat broke, left an estate worth $50 million.

William Ralston didn't fare so well. On August 26, 1875, the Bank of California closed its doors. Ralston, its president, had misspent bank assets. Rather than face the music, he took a fatal swim in San Francisco Bay.

William Sharon, by now a United States senator, gathered his board of directors. Within five days, they'd raised enough money to reopen the bank. Sharon himself chipped in $1 million. Anxious investors sighed relief. That crisis solved, a bigger one loomed.

The Virginia City Fire

October 26, 1885. At 6 a.m. inside a little boardinghouse, a brawl erupted. One of the men overturned a lantern. *Poof!* Flames swallowed the place whole.

Neighboring buildings had wooden siding, floors, and shingles. Everything was tinder-dry. Nevada autumns don't see much rain.

But they do hear the wail of the Washoe zephyr. The terrible wind blew hurricane force that day. According to DeQuille, it carried "sheets of wallpaper, blazing shingles, and a great shower of fiery missiles of all kinds."

51

Alarms sounded. The pumpers arrived. Courageous firemen did their best. But no amount of water could slow the flames. "The whole face of the mountain," wrote DeQuille, "seemed a sea of fire."

It was all over in six hours. Churches. Hotels. The Bank of California. The V&T depot. Both newspaper buildings. Piper's Opera House. Clubs. Saloons. City Hall. Homes. Two thousand buildings were swept away on waves of fire.

Piper's Opera House

Six people died. Hundreds were left homeless. Yet the spirit that built Virginia City rebuilt her right away. Aid poured in. Food, clothing, and lumber arrived the very next morning. Day and night, the hammers flew. Life in Virginia City began anew.

Brick buildings replaced wooden claptraps. An improved pipeline carried water. Three hospitals, four banks, and six churches were built. Mackay himself rebuilt the Catholic church in brick. A silver bell and cross adorned the steeple.

One high school and three grammar schools taught 2,200 children. Those kids had plenty of recreation too. In winter, they sledded or skated

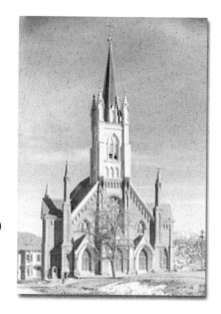

on frozen millponds. In summer, they hunted, hiked, swam, or rode ponies.

Families often rode the V&T to Washoe Valley. There, at the Bowers' Mansion resort, they picnicked in the cool meadowland. Sometimes they caught a coach to Tahoe. At the fine Glenbrook Hotel, they could board a steamboat for a lake cruise.

In 1876, the Comstock Lode peaked. The population reached its all-time high of 23,000. That meant 49 percent of all Nevadans lived in Virginia City. The Con Virginia and California mines reached top output. The two produced over $30 million that year alone.

And then the slide began—gentle at first. Even the Big Bonanza could not go on forever.

Virginia City

Chapter 9

A Tarnished Legacy

The Comstock Lode Runs Dry

Virginia City's spectacular boom ended with a thud. At 1,550 feet, the Con Virginia narrowed. At 1,650 feet, it simply quit. A few minor strikes renewed **optimism**. But by 1880, everyone knew *borrasca* had returned for good. The Comstock Lode had given her all.

Production fell. Unemployment climbed. By the end of 1877, some 2,000 men had lost their jobs. But mining continued elsewhere. So people left Virginia City in search of new dreams.

Virginia City's lavish lifestyle continued for a while. In October 1879, General Ulysses S. Grant arrived. He came by way of Sutro's tunnel. It had been completed only the year before. He toured the deep mines.

The town put on a show. From the balcony of the International Hotel, Grant watched a grand parade. Civil War veterans (both North and South), firemen, drill teams, and war-painted Paiutes marched by. Then came three days of speeches, banquets, and bonfires. It was Virginia City's last hurrah.

The major players moved on. Their money, indeed, built San Francisco. E. J. "Lucky" Baldwin (Ophir mine), B. F. Sherwood (Union mine), Fair, Mackay, Sharon, Sutro. All invested Nevada silver in Bay Area real estate. Today, San Francisco streets bear their names.

Others went east or south. Darius Mills chose New York City. There, he founded the *Herald Tribune.* Senator John Jones bought into a southern California silver mine. His money built Santa Monica.

Those left in Virginia City struggled to stay afloat. Stock market **manipulation** became common practice. As production dropped off, so did share prices. Some people bought stocks for as little as five cents. Then they'd announce a major strike was about to happen. Prices jumped. They sold the stocks and lit out before investors realized the information was false.

Others *salted* their claims by mixing a little rich ore with poor. Then the mines seemed to be worth more. But it was just another shady way to boost stock prices.

A few made **legitimate** profits by milling low-grade ore. Much had been tossed aside in favor of richer deposits. In 1883, Senator Jones leased the Con Virginia. Within six months, he made $300,000 in low-grade ore. Such efforts continued well into the 1890s.

But deep mining was dead. Mt. Davidson had given its heart—the Big Bonanza. Left behind was a giant hollow, supported by rotting timbers.

In 1881, the Consolidated Virginia mine caught fire. The tunnels were sealed and allowed to burn. When water seeped in, everything collapsed. As the ground settled, the mountain cracked open. Parts of Virginia City slid downhill.

The rest slipped quietly into history books. What stands today wears the past like faded jeans.

Yesterday, Today, Tomorrow

The Comstock Lode's story is silver. But its **legacy** is tarnished. Miners, millers, and lumbermen dug, crushed, and cut without any thought to the future. The hillsides surrounding Virginia City still wear mostly sage. The same is true for the once-lush valleys below.

Lake Tahoe was **reforested**. But mostly one type of pine was planted. It was chosen because it grew fast. But it doesn't like drought. Dry years are common in northern Nevada. An eight-year spell in the 1980s weakened the trees. Bark beetles took over. Tahoe's forests are now dying.

Cyanide and arsenic were used in the milling process. Both poisons **saturated** the dirt and washed into local water sources.

Of more concern is mercury. When the silver played out, the mills disappeared. But piles of tailings loaded with mercury remained. Over time, they mixed with the soil. And then they washed into the river, streams, and Washoe Lake.

Over 7,000 tons of mercury spilled into the Carson River alone. A hundred years of precipitation (or lack of it) have moved the **sediment**. But the years haven't cleansed it.

Virginia City with piles of tailings in the foreground

In wet years, the river overflows its banks. In dry years, the lake recedes. If either happens, mercury moves along with silt or dust. It settles wherever Mother Nature puts it.

Mercury travels up the food chain. Some grasses filter it. But most absorb it. Bugs eat **contaminated** grass. Fish eat bugs. Birds or people eat fish. Problems arise. Like most heavy metals, mercury can damage the kidneys and liver. In higher concentrations, it affects the brain. In rare cases, it kills.

The federal standard for safe mercury levels in fish is 1 part per million (ppm). In 1998, Carson River catfish measured 12 ppm. They pose a danger, both to people and the **raptors** that eat them.

Mercury occurs naturally as a liquid. But like water, it continuously **evaporates**. When temperatures rise, the liquid-to-gas process speeds up. The vapor rises. Mercury vapor can settle close to the source. Or it can stay in the air for years. The wind may carry it a great distance. And, eventually, what goes up must come down.

Mae Gustin is a researcher for the University of Nevada, Reno (UNR). "Airborne mercury is stored in the atmosphere," she explained. "Reactions to **ozone** make it settle. This can happen anywhere. For instance, there are lakes in the Midwest where you can't eat the fish [because of the mercury levels]. With no direct source of mercury, it has to come from the air."

The most likely source—Nevada mining.

The Carson River is a federal **Superfund** site. But a cleanup may do more harm than good. "Certain **restoration** projects, like wetlands, encourage the formation of **methyl mercury**," said Gustin. "This is the most toxic kind because your body can't flush it out. Instead, it builds up in the tissues."

A team of UNR researchers is studying the best way to deal with the situation. They agree a cleanup may not be possible.

The lesson of the Comstock Lode is powerful. Let's learn from it. What we do today can affect the world tomorrow. We only have one planet. Her resources are limited. We must take care of those that remain.

Glossary

abolitionist   person in favor of freeing slaves

amalgam   combination of elements

annually   yearly

arsenal   place to store weapons

ascend   to rise

assay   to estimate the worth of ore

bends   sometimes fatal condition caused by rapid change in air pressure. Symptoms include breathing difficulties, pains, paralysis, and collapse.

billiards   games played on a rectangular table by driving small balls against one another or into pockets; similar to pool

bonanza   exceptionally rich, large mineral deposit

bought	bribed; put on the payroll of someone interested in controlling how the judge would rule
braggart	person who boasts loudly
capitalist	person who has money invested in a business
chemistry	science that deals with the structure and properties of substances
cholera	disease of humans and animals. Symptoms include diarrhea and severe pain in the stomach and intestines.
clear-cut	to remove all trees in a stand of timber
Conestoga	large canvas-topped wagon named after Conestoga, Pennsylvania, where the wagons were made
contaminate	to make unfit for use
depression	period when many people are out of work and there is little money to spend
duel	fight with weapons fought between two persons in the presence of witnesses
engineer	person who uses science and math to make useful things
evaporate	to change into a gas
extract	to take out by a physical or chemical process
fictional	made-up
flume	inclined chute for a stream of water
foreclose	to take away a property when payments are not made
forty-niner	person who took part in the California gold rush in 1849
franchise	special privilege or right to do something
gallery	underground level; passageway created by mining
gang	group of people whose actions are unlawful and antisocial
geologist	person who studies the history of the earth and its life by examining rocks
hung	unable to come to a decision or verdict
isthmus	narrow strip of land that connects two larger land areas

legacy	something received from the past
legitimate	lawfully gained
manipulation	change by unlawful means
mason	skilled worker who builds with stone or brick
methyl mercury	toxic compound of mercury that, through pollution, builds up in living organisms
mineralogy	science dealing with minerals and their properties
monopoly	exclusive control or ownership of a business activity
mother lode	principle vein of a mining region
optimism	favorable outlook; hope
ozone	reactive form of oxygen that is in the atmosphere naturally
pick	heavy wooden-handled iron or steel tool pointed at one or both ends
placer	water or glacial deposit containing particles of a valuable mineral such as gold
play out	end; have nothing more to give
porphyry	fine-grained rock containing large crystals; quartz
prejudice	judgment or opinions based on race, religion, gender, or character differences
raptor	bird of prey
reclaim	obtain from a waste product
reforest	replant a forest with seedlings or young trees
restoration	act of returning to a former condition
saturate	to fill completely to the point where no more can be added or absorbed
scribbling	handwritten note
secessionist	person who supported a new nation formed by the Southern states that separated from the United States
sediment	matter that settles to the bottom of a liquid

seed money	money used to set up a new business
seismic	relating to a vibration of the earth, usually caused by an earthquake
slurry	watery mixture of matter that won't dissolve
squat	to settle on property without right, title, or payment of rent
stamp mill	place in which ore is crushed
stock	certificate that shows percentage of ownership in a business
strongbox	box that held valuables that were being shipped. Often the boxes contained payroll for railroad workers or other money being transferred from one bank to another.
subterranean	below the surface of the earth
Superfund	fund set up by the federal government to clean up hazardous materials left behind by businesses/industries. Some 1,250 sites have be selected for cleanup. To make the list, the site has to pose definite risks to people or the environment.
surveyor	person who measures and determines the form, extent, and position of something such as a piece of land
tailing	waste separated in the preparation of grain or ore
terrace	to build on ledges cut into a hillside
tetanus	infectious disease caused by a bacteria. Symptoms include spasms of the muscles of the jaw; often called lockjaw.
transatlantic	going across the Atlantic Ocean
ventilation	system of providing fresh air
way station	stopping or resting place between major stops on a line of travel
winze	steeply inclined passageway in a mine
zephyr	west wind

Index